What I Know About Jesus

A Conversation with

APOSTLE MARTHA V. GREEN

Translated by Camille Boyd

What I Know About Jesus

Copyright ©2019 by Martha V. Green

All rights reserved. No part of this book may be reproduced, copied, stored or transmitted in any form or by any means – graphic, electronic, or mechanical, including photocopying, recording, or information storage and retrieval systems without the prior written permission of Martha V. Green or HOV Publishing except where permitted by law.

Unless otherwise noted, Scripture is taken from the King James Version. Copyright © 1982 by Thomas Nelson, Inc. Used by permission. All rights reserved.

HOV Publishing a division of HOV, LLC.
www.hovpub.com, hopeofvision@gmail.com

Cover Design: HOV Design Solutions
Editor: Amy Owens for Clarity Communication

A Conversation with Apostle Martha V. Green
Translated by Camille Boyd.

Write the Apostle Martha V. Green at: lraper@snet.net

For more information about special discounts for bulk purchases, please visit www.hovpub.com

ISBN 978-1-942871-72-9

10 9 8 7 6 5 4 3 2 1
Printed in the United States of America

About The Author

Apostle Martha V. Green has served as Pastor of St. Mary's Free Will Baptist Church in New Haven, CT for 46 years. She has also mentored many churches in New Haven, Connecticut and around the country. She is a devoted mother, sister, grandmother of 5, great grandmother of 21, great great grandmother of 2, and great great great grandmother of 1. Apostle Green Loves Jesus and this book tells of what she has found to be true about the King of Kings and the Lord of Lords.

Table of Content

Forward

This beautiful day was one I will never forget. It was a cloudy overcast day that was saturated with grace for the appointed time when wisdom was to be released from God through Apostle Martha Green, my Auntie in Love. It was just a bit more special this day because she was speaking about her love for God and the wisdom, He so generously imparted into her life became crystal clear before my eyes.

Apostle Green's words represent life, love, and the power of God to energize, sustain, empower, and rejuvenate us through every season. I encourage you to take a deep drink of the words she offers; they have resulted from her wins, trials, and her relationship of love with God the Father, Son Jesus, and the Holy Spirit.

As I write, I am committed to ponder and meditate, and make these words-of-wisdom my own. It is with assurance in my heart that I say that every one of us will one day need these words, stories, and reports of miracles in good seasons, as well as in those seasons of great challenge. *Thy Kingdom come, thine will be done.*

This book represents a variety of interviews with Apostle Martha Green and her daughter, Elder Lillie Dale Raper. You will find it filled with questions, laughter, conversation, and keys that will unlock a personal journey for you and the Holy Father.

Apostle Martha V. Green is the pastor of St. Mary's Unison Free Will Baptist Church in New Haven, Connecticut. She recently celebrated her 96th birthday while writing this book, that gives a bird's eye view of a life lived with a specific assignment from God, a "*charge to keep and a God to glorify.*"

Camille Boyd-

Author of Jesus in the Schools,
Be Kind Not Mean

What I Know About Jesus

A Conversation with

APOSTLE MARTHA V. GREEN

Translated by Camille Boyd

Chapter 1

Relationship Conversations with Apostle Martha V. Green

My mother was Hattie Boyd and I loved her so! We were close and she loved St. Mary's Church. I was raised by my grand-mother Mamie White in North Carolina. I didn't let the fact that I was raised by grandma cause me to think of my mother in any other way. My mother was my mother, and my grandmother was my grandmother. I think that's why I am still here at 96-years old! *Honor thy mother and thy father and thy days shall be long upon the land which the Lord thy God giveth thee.*[1]

My mother and I were very close and she loved the church! Oh, how she loved the church! As a daughter, I stuck with my mother and she stuck with me. Momma came to me once; she had a dream that there was a storm in the church. There were strong winds and rain and some were leaving out of the church but I, in her dream remained hanging on to a pole in the dream. Through the storm, I hung on! Momma told me that some would leave the church but I would be okay. I remembered this dream she had and never forgot her words.

The day that momma passed, she told my sister Predency (Daniels), "Tell Martha I

---

[1] Exodus 20:12

have to go now." I took it to mean she was encouraging me to continue my assignment to see souls saved and love the church. That is just what I did!

I want you all to read Joshua chapter 1:13 and Deuteronomy 6. You will see they are connected. *As I was with Moses, so I will be with you.*[2]

God was with me so many times. I am brought back to thinking of the time in my life when I believe I had left my body. I was gone! My daughter Lillie kept calling 'MAMA... MAMA…MAMA!' The last time she yelled out '*Mama are you with me?*' It was the right word. ***The right word at the right time can bring life.***

---

[2] Joshua 1:5 portion of the verse

In life there are things we count as simple; like breath, but in reality it is great. I've learned and encourage others to relax and count the cost at the end of a day, to see the evidence of what God has done that day. Is there evidence of His answer? Tell the Lord thank you!

This is my prayer now. I want God to teach me how to pray, I want more of Jesus!

Love Note: The right word at the right time can bring life.

Reflections:______________________________

____

____

____

____

____

Chapter 2

The Beginning

Apostle Martha Green was born in Pitt County North Carolina in 1923 as the third of ten children. She grew up in her grandmother, Mamie White's house. This is story of her beginning.

Apostle, what was it like growing up in your grandmother's house as the third child?

My grandmother was a midwife, when she went to attend to a mother, I had to be the head of the house. At this time, I learned many things; how to cook and how to take care of the others. My grandmother would stay three or four days while awaiting the birth of a child. At that point I was about 11 or 12-years old. Ethel was the oldest but I was the one left in charge of the children younger than me. When I look back, that was a God thing because I was trusted to be in charge and care for the younger kids. School was not the priority; I could only go to school for a half day. In the morning I would attend school for my lessons and in the afternoon, I had to work as a sharecropper, but I liked it. The life I lived then taught me how to be a lady. I learned what responsibility was, making sure the children ate, were dressed, and stayed out of harm's way. I remember we had to have prayer every Sunday morning before breakfast. Everyone had to be at the table and I had to read the scripture and then we would have prayer. My grandmother was a praying woman and my grandfather was a praying man. My grandfather's name was Dan White.

My grandmother not only was a midwife, but a mother of the church. She attended a missionary church and helped others bring children into the world was part of her mission. I grew up going to church at *St.* Peter's. We had to walk to church and it was the demand of our grandparents to get to Sunday School. You worked all week in the fields and cared for the children and then on Sunday you would get up and have prayer and go to church. Now you can see I grew up in church. St. Peter's church was a joy! There was not a rug on the floor, or many instruments like churches today. We had an organ and foot pattin'. Our church had family but it was a community church where people would gather and worship God. From my earliest memory, I always wanted to do something related to caring for the church. I wanted to hang around the church. Once I was grown, I lived awhile with my mother, stepfather, and my youngest sister Predency. At that time, I would get on a tree stump and preach!

Did you have any members of your church on the stump? (laughter)

My sister 'Dency' (Predency) was my member! I would get on the stump and preach with fire like I heard so many other preachers do before me. You know, I would get up there and go, “HaaaH”!

That was a pretty lofty goal for a woman during that time in the Baptist Church wasn’t it?

No not really! You see I was not thinking about the outcome, just about preaching. What was in me had to come out.

What were you preaching about? (Laughter was uproarious!)

I know I was preaching about God. You can ask 'Dency' she remembers me on the stump!

Where did you go from there in your development in church?

Well, I was an usher first at St. Peter's. Sometimes, I would follow granddaddy. We would be on our way and pass by St. Peter's and go to a sanctified church. It was a big difference from St. Peter's. They would sing and shout and praise God in a big way. St. Peter's was dry and you couldn't go in there doing that. You could go to that sanctified church and have a good time. My grandfather was a member of St. Peter's but he was more of an outwardly praiser than they were. He was always looking for more of God. The people of St. Peter's saw that he was looking for more and they didn't like him. I would follow granddaddy because I had a thirst for more. There is more!

Now in your life, fast forward, you were now a lady. Did you marry?

Yes, I got married and that definitely made a difference in my life. However, the family I married into didn't share the same Christian values and beliefs, causing me to eventually stray away from attending church regularly, participating, and being active in the church. It was not long before I divorced

Lillie's father. On one side of the river where I lived was Greenville, NC and the other side of the river was Simpson and Blackjack, this was like a dividing line. When I went over the river to Simpson and Blackjack that is where I met my future husband Willie Jessie. He was Lillie's stepfather. Willie Jessie was nice; everybody had their ways but he was a good provider and strict on some things.

Now about your call to preach, can you tell us?

Well, I got my call in 1963. I had come to Connecticut in 1953. In 1953 I joined Pitts Chapel in New Haven and continued ushering like I was in my home church Sweet Hope in

Greenville, NC. When I came to Pitts Chapel I loved to usher and I sang in the church choir #1 and #2. In 1963 when I got my call it was funny. It was funny because I seen so many fail. There were three pleas I put before the Lord to make sure this is what I was called to do. The third time He showed me what I would consider to be woods and water. The water was in the center. I had to get across the water. I was wearing white and the Spirit said stretch out your hands. I wasn't flying in the air like a bird, no I was flying just over the water. When He took me up, I saw heaven. He said, if you don't do my will you won't get there! After this encounter I was sure I was called to preach. Next, I had to go to my husband Willie Jessie, then my pastor. They were in total agreement and the way was already made. My first sermon in 1963 was “As I Was With Moses, So I Will Be With You” that was Joshua 1:5. Through the scripture and prayer I knew I would not be defeated by any man! These were my sending orders that kept me many days. There were many challenges and stuff I had to face with both men and women in the ministry.

Love Note: Are you thinking of the outcome or are you fixed on what God called you to do?

____

____

____

____

____

____

____

____

Chapter 3

The Call

We continue the interview of Apostle Green about her path following God as a woman and daughter of God in the Gospel.

Apostle you had your call that kept you . What was it like being a woman preaching the Gospel in the 1970s?

Well, I went on what I know God had revealed to me. He said He would be with me and that is exactly what I believed. There were still obstacles that had to come my way, I was rejected, talked about in hurtful ways. One person asked me how could I preach when I couldn't even read! I lost many friends because I didn't let them dictate to me because I had a calling. God said He would be with me and when bad things happened, I would remember what God said. As rejection came, doors were opening up at the same time. Many denominations called upon me to minister to them. They made requests for me to perform weddings and other ministry duties. At one time they would not allow any Baptist preacher in the Church of God in Christ, I went in there too. Muslims also invited me, and opened the doors, and welcomed me. There were some doors open and some shut. I promised the Lord that I would hold on to Him until the end. I have kept that promise and

THAT is a GOD thing. If God wasn't with me there would be no way in the world to keep this promise that I hold on to today.

Tell me about the start of the church St. Mary's where you pastor today?

In 1973 while sitting under the leadership of Pastor Austin Atkinson for ten years, my initial sermon, as I said, was in 1963. The wait for ten years, was coming to an end at Pitt's Chapel. My Pastor, Reverend Atkinson, was going out of town and he left me in charge. My first sermon preaching at Pitt's Chapel, a soul, Maybell Washington, came to Christ. Maybell is still a member of St. Mary's today.

At Pitt's Chapel, the Pastor put me in charge of a three-night revival. Everyone rejected me during this process. The last night, that Friday of the revival an entire family came to Christ. During revival back then people had a desire to be saved, they would come sit on the bench, *the mourners bench.* I must say, IT WENT THE WAY THE Lord wanted it to go! If it had gone the way people wanted, nothing would happen. I couldn't get any help, but God was in the midst. That last night God came in and showed who was in control by saving the entire family. The one that first got saved in the family is now Pastoring her own church on Derby Avenue, her name is Overseer Willie May Clayton.

So, your apostolic gifting was active back then?

Yes, many people have come through the doors of St. Mary's and many miracles have been seen.

Tell me more about how St. Mary's came about?

One Sunday, the Spirit spoke to me about pastoring. It was strange but after I pondered the word and it got in my spirit, I went to seeking members. You can't have a church without members. God gave me Eddie, Betty, Florence, and May. He gave me seven members to set up the church. In order to set up a church you have to have seven officers; mothers, deacons, a secretary, a treasurer, and trustees. God gave me all of them. Two of these people are living and the rest have passed away. Florence named the church, Eddie Daniels was the first trustee, and he is still there now. As time went on, God kept adding on to the church. God filled all the offices and my mother was the first mother of the church. We went on Grand Avenue, and fixed that place up, and it was small. God kept adding to His church until we had to leave there because we had outgrown the space. He sent us on Beers Street for three years. We fixed up the building on Goffe Street which was originally an old auto repair shop. When we moved from Beers Street, I had an usher that passed that Sunday. When we went to see him, we had just gotten the mortgage; that's when Betty, another member, died. It was bittersweet! I started the church in 1973, I had three members born again on that day in 1973 when I established the church. God knows I have seen so many miracles. There are so many things that happened with three, I was born in 1923,

I'm the third child, I did my initial sermon in '63, started the church in '73, and 3 members were born-again on that day. Wow! He planted me on threes.

Love Note: You must love your assignment or else you won't sacrifice for something you don't love.

Chapter 4

Work Life

Although Apostle Green pastored St. Mary's church for 46 years, that was not the extent of her service in the New Haven community. Martha's work as a child with the responsibility of her family and share-cropping, helped her walk into her call to care for others with the right attitude. Apostle Green stayed focused on her assignments and let God take care of the outcomes.

I worked at Minor's in the factory portion of the dress shop for two to three years. We made children's clothes and supplied the dresses for Eli's dress shop located in downtown New Haven. I enjoyed the work and the nice people. It helped me clothe my grandchildren. Every job I enjoyed, I always wanted to go. I was on time and never let the weather stop me. I always enjoyed my jobs.

Apostle I haven't heard you say there was a job that you didn't enjoy. That most certainly is a God thing!

Yes, it was a God thing, I enjoyed all my work. Right before we opened St. Mary's in 1973, I started working at the Veterans' Administration (VA). When I first went there it was a bit strange because the people there were not too friendly, I saw it as a job. I took my eye off the people and put it on the responsibility of the work. Therefore, I loved the work at the VA! I built up my time, 22 years to be exact. I would have worked there longer but it was hard to work with the people of the church as a pastor and work at the VA at the same time.

What kind of work did you do at the Veterans Administration?

The VA position changed as I worked my way up through different jobs. I worked on the laundry table. Different items would be taken on to a truck from Newington to West Haven. The laundry had to be washed, folded, and put on the truck lined up by two hundred. There were pajama tops and bottoms that were laundered. We had a machine that would run the sheets and pillowcases. When they were finished, there were workers who folded them and then we placed them on the truck. I worked on the uniform side as well. Each worker had to do a month rotation on the pressing side for the uniforms and the "flat work side." When I was working on the uniform side that's where I received my promotion. My next step was as a leader on the floor and I was responsible for the people who were doing the work and their productivity.

I can see where you were once again chosen to be a leader. Did you enjoy this as well?

Yes, I did!

When did it become a challenge to pastor and perform your duties at the VA?

After 22 years, I came out of the VA at the age of 63. I knew the season was changing because the people were changing. There was a lot of jealousy that caused problems. I knew that I couldn't do the two things. I went and talked to my boss and he said I could retire at 63, that's when I made my choice. I did not come out depending on the church. I did not take any salary until the church was paid for.

Wow! For you to not take a salary until the church was paid for, that's a God thing.

That's the love of God, ain't it?

Yes Apostle, indeed it is!

As a pastor you had to be concerned about the church. The first anniversary celebration...the gift they gave me from the church, I gave every penny back. I was not depending on the church; I was depending on God and we survived and God did it.

Was there any point along this journey that you had a doubt?

No, because some things rose up but did I have a doubt in God? I went through discouragement but I know God said it and He was going to work it out. Then when you have people to work with your dream, the plan can go forward and work better.

You had seven people to work with when you founded St. Mary's Church?

Yes, you need a team of people working on the same line. There has to be a relationship between the team. Doing this (pastoring a church) you have to have faith in what you're doing. If you have doubters saying you don't have the money for this vision, it brings confusion. Money can be a problem for people like that and you shouldn't fool yourself, they will make that plan harder. You have to have people that are not looking at money but looking at the will of God. Everything belongs to God.

These are people you didn't handpick, God sent them your way.

The ones that went with the vision, yes God sent them. That bunch of people were the best, they were workers that were committed.

You need workers and you don't need doubters.

Workers have faith in God and not the money! For example, at St. Mary's we worked as a family in many ways. In the 46 years we outgrew several locations and had to move. When we planned to move to 49 Goffe Street, it was not a church. The property was an old auto repair shop. God sent me a vision. In *this* location, instead of repairing cars, we would be repairing souls. The men of St. Mary's along with Union Temple's deacons (a church we had friendship with), Deacons James Brantley and Pearlie Pearson, completed the renovation to transform it to our place of worship.

Love Notes: *"It's not what you see, it's what you know."* Apostle Green

The word of God is true and what you know. What things are you "seeing" that need to be subject beneath what you know?

Chapter 5

What I've Learned

(As told by Apostle Green's daughter Lillie)

This book isn't about me. It's about my mother and the core of what she believes. It shows that anyone can have their desires come to fruition when God is the center of their lives. Her life is exemplary because of what she does. To sum up what my mother, Pastor Green, is about and the source of who she is—it's *a God thing*. Her life is an example of what can happen in your life when it becomes *a God thing* for you. My mother demonstrates the fruits of the Spirit in every part of her life. She is loving, extremely kind, and she always goes the extra mile for others. She is an example of how we all can live our lives for God.

When my mother received her call to the ministry, she faced opposition and many challenges. In 1963, women were not necessarily welcomed as preachers or leaders. During that time, she was serving at Pitts Chapel and the pastor entrusted her to organize and preside over a revival for the church and the community. This was her first revival! Even though few people were willing to help, God gave her the strength and the anointing to carry through with it. The result was the manifestation of the true love of God. At this first revival, a family received Christ and the Lord saw fit to call one of the children, Pastor Willie Mae Clayton, to ministry.

In 1973, my mother was called to pastor St. Mary's. Her first challenge was to get seven people to form a church. She made many sacrifices in order to carry out the vision God gave her. For 16 years I saw how God provided whatever was needs to keep the church going until it was paid off. My mother never accepted a salary, that was a God thing. Her heart for God's church allowed her to give more than she could have ever received. On the occasion that the congregation gave her a gift, she would donate it right back to the church.

Whenever anything needed to be done, my mother always exemplified a true servant leader. She never asked anyone to do a task that she was not willing to do herself. My mother was frequently at the hospital visiting the sick. God's heart for His people motivated her to visit those in need any time of day or night. I recall a time when a dear church member who had been diagnosed with cancer was gravely ill. Although he was unable to speak, my mother sat at his bedside all day. In the evening, when she was ready to leave, this very sick man sat up in his bed and spoke very clear words to her from his heart, "God bless you." On that night he went home to be with the Lord.

Often times people will do just enough to get by. This is not at all how my mother operates! There are numerous times that I have witnessed her go the extra mile and I know it has not been by her own strength. Her life has been a testimony to the scripture, "I can do all things through Christ which strengthens me."[3] I vividly remember when my mother was diagnosed with breast cancer. Although the diagnosis was grim and she had to go through surgery and radiation, I knew God would bring her through. Every morning that she would go to the McGiveny Cancer Center, my mother would dress as if she was going to a presidential gala. While undergoing the grueling process of radiation she would encourage other patients enduring the same, or worse. Her courage, strength, and grace throughout this process showed me all that God could do in the midst of a storm. On Sundays, Pastor Green donned her robe and let God use her to preach a fiery message. All the

---

[3] Philippians 4:13

while, St. Mary's members never knew the challenges their pastor was experiencing.

Pastor Apostle Green is an amazing example to me of a woman of God, a mother, and a loving grandmother. My husband, our children Joyce, Janet, Denise, Nina, and beloved son Kevin (now deceased), and our entire family have been blessed by the example Apostle Martha Green has set.

Love Notes: When the Word goes forth you ought to see some evidence in your life. What evidence of God's goodness can you see in your life?

____

____

____

____

What I've Learned

Chapter 6

Tell the Lord Thank you!

The gratitude that marks Apostle Martha Green's life is obvious in one of her most famous, frequently used statements. She rears her head back and beckons you to join her in one accord, tell the Lord thank you! She has many reasons to thank the Lord as we all do. Elder Lillie Raper, myself, (Minister Camille Boyd) and Apostle Green engaged in conversation about the record of God's goodness. This chapter explains in further detail the God who raises the dead, raised her!

I have been at the bedside of many sick people and prayed for them. Once I prayed for a man that was told by the doctors, he was very ill and near death. I prayed for that man and he was completely healed. He was discharged from the hospital and was able to travel after that. I have witnessed the gospel to people on their deathbeds. Death starts from the foot where your foot gets cold and progresses up the body.

Apostle Green herself was revived from death at one point in her life. According to Lillie, her mother was always active. She was in her eighties when she decided to travel alone to North Carolina to visit relatives. When she returned home after the travel, she wasn't feeling well. They called the doctor who suggested it might be the flu. Lillie decided to bring Apostle to the emergency room when all of a sudden, this thing came over her! I got the chair and suddenly she jerked forward and she was on the floor. Her body was jerking and moving uncontrollably. Yelling her name repeatedly, "Mama!" Apostle Green could hear but not respond, she was gone! The last time Lillie yelled frantically "Mama are you with me?" Apostle could feel herself coming back to her body and eventually she responded, "Yeah." She loosened her bowels and her clothes had the smell of death.

Later, they found out that on the bus trip, blood clots had developed in her legs from sitting stationary for a long period of time. The real blessing was that this emergency held off until she got home.

Apostle Green shared, “When I was loading the bus, I wanted to tell my family ‘Goodbye, I might not see you again.’ I wanted to tell them but I didn’t speak it. When Lillie was calling Mama, I heard her but couldn’t answer. When I was able to answer I felt myself coming back into my body. In the ambulance they were asking me questions and I couldn’t answer. Apparently at that point I had no pulse. “I fell in the bathroom but God didn’t let me hit my head. Through many toils and snares, I have already come.”

When she arrived at the hospital the doctor recommended a medication for the blood clots. This medication was a high risk because there was potential of an aneurysm occurring. Lillie gave the doctor approval to administer the medication. Another miracle occurred in this process; no blood clots were found in her bodily secretions.

Apostle, was there another miracle when your life was spared by God?

Oh yes! Lillie and I were hit broad-side and they knocked our car in a snowbank. The airbag deployed and hit Lillie in the face. The airbag on my side didn't discharge at all. We were coming from a hairdresser appointment travelling homebound on Kimberly Avenue when the car came barreling off the highway out of control. It knocked us into the snowbank near an underpass.

When you see me praising God, I have a reason to! Another time Lillie was on her way to work when she was hit by an 18-wheeler. The truck hit the back door and took off the rear-view mirror but it skipped Lillie. The Lucky Ducky truck was blessed by God. The driver reported that he never saw the car.

When you stop and look back on all He has brought you through. You have to remind yourself when problems come, you have to tell yourself of the goodness of God. If you go on in life and everyone loves you all the time you wouldn't learn anything, hardship teaches valuable lessons.

Lillie: "When I first received Christ and came into the church, I thought it was all smooth sailing. Apostle thought it was going to be smooth sailing too. I thank God for what I learned. You got to know the source and whose side you are on. You must go through trials and tribulations. You learn not to carry your feelings on your shoulders."

APOSTLE Green thought to name this book WHAT I KNOW ABOUT JESUS

It's not what I think, it's what I know. The encounter I had with Jesus! The encounter and the experience that I had with Jesus in my life, I learned He's the great I AM!

Every one of the prophets, they have experienced miracles of the impossible with Him. When you have an experience with a person, you really know who they are. When you have an experience with the Lord in your life, you are growing and maturing. There's a lot in that experience, love, peace, healing, joy...whatever you need. What is He to you, author, finisher, savior?

The book that God gave you Camille, *Jesus in The Schools,* someone can read it and get saved. Your experience helps you to get the experience. There are so many purposes in everything He's doing. Each of us has to have our own experience.

Apostle, can you give an example of what you are referring to?

People are constantly wondering how I became an Apostle and how I was ordained for such an assignment. For example, I was asked to speak at a funeral with many important people. Many continue to wonder why I was chosen for my apostleship. God birthed the spirit of apostle just like I was having a baby. I was on Lawrence street, it was at a service, the spirit came out of me. The office of Apostle is not by man, it's by God. I am taking that for myself because I know God called me to it.

The path God chose for me was different, I didn't sit down and have man lay a hand on me. This assignment is not of men, but of God. When He birthed that spirit, I knew that it came from God. Once I was listening to a program years ago and they were talking about birthing a spirit. Although it was many years ago, I pondered it for a long time. That spirit of a bishop or apostle has to be birthed.

Lillie: Otherwise you are just riding shot gun, (With uproarious laughter!)

Apostle is there anything else you really want people to know?

When you have been delivered, everything increases your praise, your giving of yourself, and your life. You can go farther and deeper in Christ when you are delivered. You really begin to learn about him. When deliverance happens, your experience increases in Christ.

Deliverance is a word like amazing grace! It gets rid of those things holding you back. The word delivered, you can own and its impact can go on and on. If one word can open up the floodgates, it is *delivered.* No more chains holding me because I'm delivered. Delivered means I am really getting stronger in the Lord.

Grace is unmerited favor, something you didn't earn. God's grace ought to make you more dutiful, more thankful, more mindful of Him because you didn't work for it! Grace makes me more grateful and thankful; it makes me want to do more. Faith and grace go together. God's grace, *grace* is a powerful word too. People don't want to give you what you earned, never mind what you didn't. God, you saw me as a wretch undone. Your love for me, your grace, I didn't love myself, but your grace! Your grace! Tender mercies are new every morning. The Bible says His grace is sufficient in your weakness. We really don't know what we have; when we have Jesus in our lives, we have power. He has the authority to speak His grace. Is anything too hard for God, is anything? That takes up the universe.

Situations have been changed! Death was on me but God changed it and gave me a longer life. He turned around my death sentence! I have seen things changed around. There was a man on his death bed the last word he said to me, "God bless you." He left the blessings of God on me. The thief on the cross, he was hanging there on the cross and grace allowed him to ask the question. Will you remember me when you get in paradise? Jesus granted him grace to invite him into paradise. Grace plays a part in your life and you don't earn it. Grace ought to make you be a better Christian. Grace doesn't give you license to sin, grace settles it! Your good works do not remedy your sin. How good are you? See yourself, and then see grace. I don't care how many good works I do. It's counted but it doesn't pay the price for my sin. God honors the good work you do! If a drunk sees an old lady going across the street, God honors his good work in helping the lady. Christ does the saving. Once you get His spirit in you, then you become like him. You ought to have his attributes if you are saved. When you have him you ought to bear what He bears. Evil doesn't flow out of you if you have the Spirit of the Lord. Jesus said he came to do the works of the

Father. There is no other name that you can be saved, but the name of Jesus! At the name of Jesus every knee has to bow and every tongue confess.

Know Jesus' power and use it for its intended purpose. Jesus is all over me! He is keeping me alive. Jesus is the strong tower. If you sit down, take the time and think about the name of Jesus. His name is above all names! As long as you live, He is showing you how better to serve him. If you go to a store and you know what they have, why go in complaining? We bring some things on ourselves by mingling with those things, people, and places that we know are not of God.

As you grow in the Lord, the things that used to affect you, now you can step through it. God can take the worst of us and make the best of us! God is a God that can change minds. God knows all things.

What more could God do for a sinful nature? No man could take the place of Jesus to redeem man. You don't love him enough to keep his commandments? The greatest commandment is love one another! I died for you! You are created in my image. In this world you have trials and tribulations but what's in your basket (your heart)? As a preacher, you are standing amongst the congregation, do you have anything in your basket to help the least?

Are you living beneath your privilege? You don't have to; God says, "My gift is here for you! God chose you for your benefit. I open the door for your opportunity."

Here is an example, Deacon James Bradley of Union Temple helped St. Mary's make a decision regarding our location. We purchased the land on Wintergreen Avenue, which was over seven acres. He said if the church was built there on Wintergreen, the people would have to be transported to church. The vision of the church on Shelton Avenue, it is on the bus line and the people came to us.

Apostle, do you have any reflections on your journey?

On July 29 Bishop Gay came to the church to preach and my mother Hattie Boyd told him to take care of me; this word was a blessing for me.

My initial sermon was titled "As I Was with Moses, I Will be with You." My life with God has been a testament to this. My Pastor, the late Dr. Bishop Austin Atkins said in your ministry you won't go lacking because people would come in as families. This was in the latter part of 1974 and today we are still receiving families in 2019. The vision is still alive!

I met the Muslim Iman Hassan at St. Mary's on Goffe Street. He wanted to meet with me so he scheduled a time and came. The relationship developed so well that the mosque family would have birthday celebrations yearly for me. For my 90th birthday celebration, there were 200 or more people with 23 churches represented as far north as Massachusetts, as far south as South Carolina.

"Endure hardness as a good soldier" you have to be able to stand up to what you face. You have to be determined. Be a good fighter. You can't be a good fighter if you are not looking for better. You have to have something in mind that you are hoping for in Christ.

You have to endure in order to see what the result is going to be. If you have something in your mind, then you will press. There's a blessing in the press! After the 46 years I have been pastoring and all the good God has done for me, it makes me want to run on! He has brought me back on the winning side. Here is my prayer for you from the book of Nehemiah. Built they the wall because the people had a mind to work. Nehemiah[4].

What I know about Jesus is a book that tells of the experience of Martha V. Green as an apostle. I pray these words of wisdom are hidden deep within your heart to be manifest for generations until the coming of Jesus Christ.

-Minister Camille Boyd

[4] Nehemiah 4:6 portion of the verse

Love Notes

Words of Wisdom from Apostle Green

- *When we pray, we pray God's will. You have to send the word to sickness to accomplish the healing.*
- *When the Word is sent out you ought to see some evidence.*
- *Do you know what you're looking for?*
- *Do you know what you have?*
- *Do you know who you are?*
- *The Word came to change you, we didn't come to change the word.*
- *We must begin to live in our privilege.*

- *In your weakest hour God will give you strength.*
- *In your failure you have to hold on. If you hold on you will reap the benefits.*
- *If you fail don't run and hide from God.*
- *You are still saved in your weakness. In my weakness God gives me strength.*
- *Have you received power over yourself?*
- *God gave you an assignment, be grateful for it and keep it with all your heart.*
- *Everything you love you will sacrifice for.*
- *I dare you to use God's word!*
- *If He gave you life, you can go through anything.*

- *The higher up you go, the less stress you have, because you are hid in Christ. Go Higher!!!*
- *It's not what you see it's what you know.*
- *Don't give up, stay in the race God gave you.*

Love Notes
Journal

Photo Gallery

Deacon Willie J. & Pastor Martha V. Green

ST. MARY'S UNISON FREEWILL BAPTIST CHURCH
Established April 1973 New Haven, CT
BEERS STREET
49 GOFFE STREET
Pastor Martha V. Green
1953
Moved To Connecticut
1963
Started Preaching
1973
Became Pastor & Founder
of
St. Mary's UFB Church
GRAND AVENUE

Apostle Green 1st Pastor Austin Atkinson

Apostle Martha V. Green with Bishop

Church Pastors and Church Mother

Deacons and Deaconess

Males Chorus

Apostle Green Sister and Brother-in-law

Apostle Green's Family

James & Lillie Raper

Apostle Green and Great Great Great Granddaughter

Apostle Green Awards

www.ingramcontent.com/pod-product-compliance
Lightning Source LLC
Chambersburg PA
CBHW070241090526
44586CB00035B/1371

* 9 7 8 1 9 4 2 8 7 1 7 2 9 *